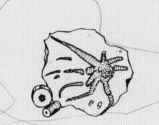

M is for Missouri

Written by Carol Greene   Illustrated by Michelle Dorenkamp

Published by GHB Publishers

GHB Publishers, L.L.C.
3906 Old Highway 94 South, Suite 300
St. Charles, MO 63304

Book cover design by Werremeyer |Floresca
Cover illustration by Michelle Dorenkamp

Manufactured in the United States of America
First Edition

10 9 8 7 6 5 4 3 2 1

Library of Congress Cataloging-in-Publication Data

Greene, Carol
M is for Missouri / Carol Greene ; illustrated by Michelle Dorenkamp
Saint Charles, Mo : GHB Publishers, c2000.
p. : ill., maps,
Includes index.

Summary: Gives an overview of the state of Missouri, including its history,
notable sights, people, and recreations.

Missouri--History--Juvenile literature.

Missouri--History.

Missouri.

I. Title   977.8--dc21   F466.3

ISBN 1-892920-26-3

"A" is for the Gateway Arch • "B" is for Daniel Boone • "C" is for George Washington Carver • "D" is for Bagnell Dam • "E" is for the Pony Express • "F" is for Eugene Field • "G" is for the Missouri Botanical Garden • "H" is for Hannibal • "I" is for Ice Cream Cone • "J" is for Scott Joplin • "K" is for Kindergarten • "L" is for Lewis and Clark • "M" is for Mastodon • "N" is for New Madrid • "O" is for the Ozarks • "P" is for Pioneer • "Q" is for Quantrill's Raiders • "R" is for River • "S" is for Dred Scott • "T" is for Harry S. Truman • "U" is for Und[...]a Ingalls Wilder • "X" is for eXtr[...]s for the Saint Louis Zoo • "A"[...]one • "C" is for George Washi[...]s for the Pony Express • "F" is[...]al Garden • "H" is for Hannibal • "I" is for Ice Cream Cone • "J" is for Scott Joplin • "K" is for Kindergarten • "L" is for Lewis and Clark • "M" is for Mastodon • "N" is for New Madrid • "O" is for the Ozarks • "P" is for Pioneer • "Q" is for Quantrill's Raiders • "R" is for River • "S" is for Dred Scott • "T" is for Harry S. Truman • "U" is for Underground • "V" is for Old Village • "W" is for Laura Ingalls Wilder • "X" is for eXtra Facts • "Y" is for the Year of the Ten Boats • "Z" is for the Saint Louis Zoo • "A" is for the Gateway Arch • "B" is for Daniel Boone • "C"

MISSOURI STATE SYMBOLS

Animal	Mule
Bird	Bluebird
Fish	Channel Catfish
Floral Emblem	Hawthorn
Fossil	Crinoid
Insect	Bee
Rock	Mozarkite
Tree	Flowering Dogwood

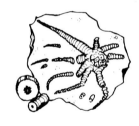

Motto	"The Welfare of the People Shall Be the Supreme Law"
Nickname	"Show-Me State"
Song	"Missouri Waltz"
State Capital	Jefferson City

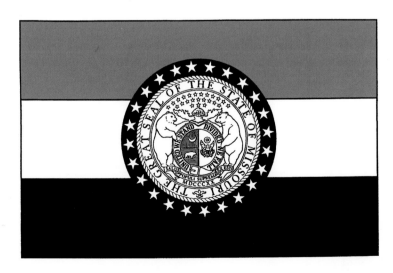

MISSOURI history

Prehistoric people may have lived in Missouri 30,000 years ago. When French explorers came in the 1600s, they met friendly Native Americans of many tribes.

The French claimed the whole Mississippi Valley for France. They called it Louisiana. Soon fur trappers, traders, and other settlers came.

In 1803, France sold the Louisiana Territory to the United States. Missouri was part of that. In 1812, it became its own territory.

Settlers took over the Native Americans' land, which caused battles. These conflicts ended in 1815. In 1821, Missouri became the 24th state.

During the Civil War, some Missourians fought for the North. Others fought for the South. Gangs of bandits hurt many people.

After the war, Missouri grew. Now farmers raise corn, soybeans, hogs, and beef cattle. Factories make cars and airplanes. Most people do jobs that help other people.

AAa is for the Gateway Arch.

St. Louis

The Gateway Arch rises 630 feet into the air beside the Mississippi River in St. Louis.

It reminds people of the brave pioneers who went west through Missouri. Tramways inside the Arch take visitors to windows at the top.

BBb
is for
Daniel Boone.

Defiance

The Nathan Boone Home in Defiance.

Daniel Boone was a famous explorer. He helped people settle in Missouri and other states. Boone died at his son's house in Defiance in 1820.

Cc is for George Washington Carver.

•Diamond

George Washington Carver grew up in Diamond.

George Washington Carver National Monument in Diamond.

8

He became a famous scientist and teacher.

He discovered hundreds of uses for peanuts, soybeans, and sweet potatoes.

Dr. Carver taught people how to be better farmers and to be kind to one another.

DDd
is for
Bagnell Dam.

Bagnell Dam

People built Bagnell Dam across the Osage River. The dam made the water back up and form the huge Lake of the Ozarks. Now many people spend their vacations at this beautiful lake.

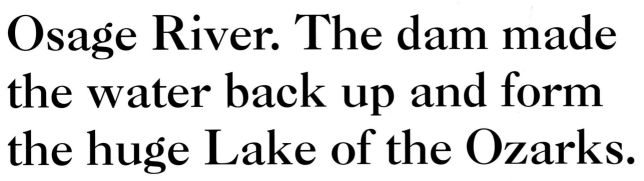

•St. Joseph

is for the Pony Express.

Above: Johnny Fry, the best-known and probably the first Pony Express rider from St. Joseph.

Right: The Patee House in 1860, when it served as the Pony Express headquarters.

In 1860 and 1861, Pony Express riders carried the mail from St. Joseph to Sacramento, California. They went almost 2,000 miles in ten days. Today you can still visit the Pony Express stables in St. Joseph.

 **is for Eugene Field.**

Eugene Field was born in a tall brick house in St. Louis.

Walsh's Row, 600 block of South Broadway, 1910. Eugene Field's house is at the far end of the row.

When he grew up, he wrote many poems for children.

Two of them are "The Sugar-Plum Tree" and "Wynken, Blynken, and Nod."

15

Gg

is for the Missouri Botanical Garden.

A huge dome called the Climatron stands at the Missouri Botanical Garden in St. Louis.

A tropical rain forest with strange, beautiful plants grows inside the Climatron. Birds, butterflies, frogs, toads, geckoes, and other tropical animals live there, too.

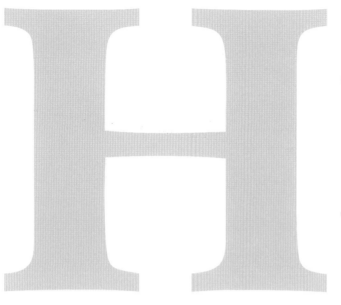

Hh

is for Hannibal.

Hannibal

Hannibal is the town on the Mississippi River where

Mark Twain's Boyhood Home and Museum in Hannibal.

author Mark Twain grew up.

Many things in his book, *The Adventures of Tom Sawyer*, really happened to Mark and his friends. You can visit places in Hannibal where the adventures took place.

**is for
ice cream
cone.**

**In 1904,
the St. Louis
World's Fair
welcomed
guests from
all over.**

Soon many of them were licking a treat that became very popular at the fair, the ice cream cone.

Some people say that the ice cream cone may have been invented at the fair, along with hot dogs and iced tea.

J j

is for Scott Joplin.

Sedalia

Scott Joplin was a famous composer and performer of ragtime music.

22

He lived in both Sedalia and St. Louis. Two of his ragtime pieces are "Maple Leaf Rag" and "The Entertainer."

KKk

is for kindergarten.

Crayon portrait
of Susan Blow.

In 1873, Susan Blow opened the first public kindergarten in the United States at St. Louis' Des Peres School. She taught all 68 children that year!

Ll is for Lewis and Clark.

St. Charles

President Thomas Jefferson sent Meriwether Lewis and William Clark to explore the west.

Lewis and Clark crossing
South Dakota
(a supplement to the
St. Louis Globe-Democrat).

26

They camped in present-day St. Charles and set out on May 14, 1804. They went all the way to the Pacific Ocean. Lewis and Clark brought back maps, journals, Native American clothes, plants, and animals, including two grizzly bears.

M

Mm

is for mastodon.

Kimmswick•

Mastodon • Mastodon • Mastodon • Mastodon • Mastodon • Mastodon • Mastodon • Mastodon

Mastodons were hairy prehistoric relatives of elephants. They are extinct now. But skeletons found near Kimmswick prove that both mastodons and elephants lived there in ancient times.

Nn
is for
New Madrid.

New Madrid

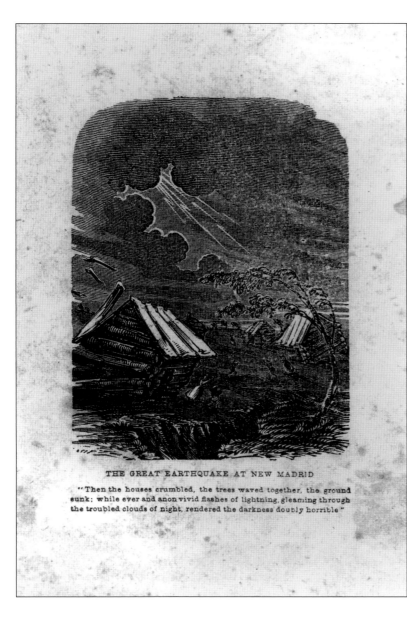

THE GREAT EARTHQUAKE AT NEW MADRID

"Then the houses crumbled, the trees waved together, the ground sunk; while ever and anon vivid flashes of lightning, gleaming through the troubled clouds of night, rendered the darkness doubly horrible"

In 1811 and 1812, fierce earthquakes hit the little town of **New Madrid** by the **Mississippi River.**

The river changed course and the town had to move. Now its first site is under the river.

Oo

is for the Ozarks.

Lake
of the
Ozarks

Ozark Mountain
Region

Ozark
Heritage
Region

Tree-covered hills and low mountains make up the area called the Ozarks.

Silver Dollar City glassblowers (from left to right) Ray Jones, Kenny Marine, and Terry Bloodworth.

Tourists visit its many caves, lakes, springs, and streams. They listen to country music in the town of Branson and watch craftspeople work at Silver Dollar City.

P

P p

is for pioneer.

Kansas City • Independence

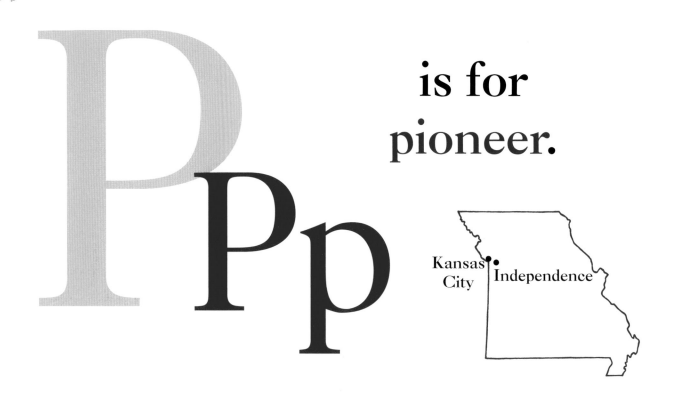

During the 1840s, many brave pioneers put together their covered wagons in Missouri.

Photo from *The Central Magazine.*

Then they stocked up with supplies and set out for the west. People in St. Joseph, Independence, Westport (now Kansas City), and other western Missouri towns helped them begin their journey.

Qq

is for Quantrill's Raiders.

• Kearney

Jesse James,
age 28.

During the Civil War, gangs of bandits from both the North and South roamed Missouri and attacked helpless people. One of the worst gangs was Quantrill's Raiders. The outlaw Jesse James, who was born in Kearney, belonged to this group of bandits.

R Rr

is for river.

The St. Louis levee in 1904.

Two important rivers flow through Missouri: the Mississippi and the Missouri. They are the longest rivers in the United States. Through the years, they have made Missouri an important center of shipping and travel.

SSs is for Dred Scott.

Dred Scott was a slave who went to court in St. Louis to win his freedom.

In 1857, the United States Supreme Court said he must remain a slave. At last, his owners gave him his freedom. But the Dred Scott case made many people angry about slavery.

T

Tt is for Harry S. Truman.

• Lamar

Harry Truman was born in Lamar. He was vice-president of the United States and became president when Franklin D. Roosevelt died in 1945. In 1948, Truman was elected to serve his own term as president.

U

Uu
is for
underground.

• Marvel Cave

Underground in Missouri are over 1,450 caves.

44

Some are huge and filled with beautiful rock formations. Marvel Cave, near Branson, has ten miles of tunnels.

Vv is for Old Village.

A very early map of St. Louis.

About 1,000 years ago, a large city called Old Village stood where St. Louis now stands. People came there to trade for pottery, jewelry, weapons, salt, and other goods. Some of the big mounds these people built still remain.

Ww
is for Laura Ingalls Wilder.

Mansfield

Laura Ingalls Wilder, age 25.

The Laura Ingalls Wilder—Rose Wilder Lane Home and Museum in Mansfield.

48

When Laura Ingalls grew up, she married Almanzo Wilder.

After a while, they moved to Rocky Ridge Farm, near Mansfield. There Laura wrote her famous *Little House* books.

Xx is for eXtra facts.

Missouri's borders touch eight states: Illinois, Kentucky, Tennessee, Arkansas, Oklahoma, Kansas, Nebraska, and Iowa.

Many men of the Osage tribe of Native Americans in Missouri were over seven feet tall.

Auguste Chouteau was in charge of the men who built the first buildings at St. Louis. At that time, he was only 13 years old.

The Springfield National Cemetery is the only cemetery where both Northern and Southern soldiers of the Civil War are buried.

• Springfield

Y Yy is for the Year of the Ten Boats.

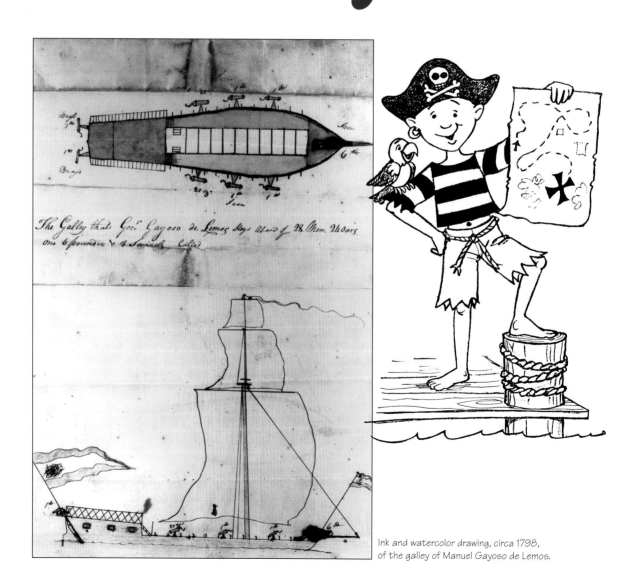

Ink and watercolor drawing, circa 1798,
of the galley of Manuel Gayoso de Lemos.

In the late 1700s, pirates kept attacking boats on the Mississippi River. Finally in 1788, crews on ten boats went up and down the river and drove the pirates away. After the Year of the Ten Boats, river towns grew much more quickly.

Zz is for the Saint Louis Zoo.

St. Louis has one of the world's finest zoos.

Workers there are trying to help endangered animals.

You can visit most parts of the zoo for free.

INDEX

SUGGESTED READINGS

Kim Simon, former owner of the children's book wholesaler Reading Express, suggests the following titles to further expand a child's library on Missouri:

Caves
> *Written by Judith Greenberg*
> *Published by Raintree*

Members of a cave expedition learn how different kinds of caves and cave formations are created in nature. They also discover what caves and cave animals are like.

Daniel Boone, Frontier Hero
> *Written by Elaine Raphael and Don Bolognese*
> *Published by Scholastic*

A biography for youngsters ages 4–8.

Mrs. Bindergarten Gets Ready for Kindergarten
> *Written by Joseph Slate and Ashley Wolff*
> *Published by Dutton*

Introduces letters of the alphabet as Miss Bindergarten gets her students ready for kindergarten.

They're Off! The Story of the Pony Express
> *Written and Illustrated by Cheryl Harness*
> *Published by Simon & Schuster*

Provides a factual, exciting, and beautifully illustrated account of the American Postal system in the 1860s, covering the origins and history of the Pony Express.

Wynken, Blynken, and Nod
> *Written by Eugene Field*
> *Published by North-South Books*

In this bedtime poem by a St. Louis author, three fishermen in a wooden shoe catch stars in their nets of silver and gold.

REFERENCES FOR TEACHERS/PARENTS

The Civil War in Missouri Day by Day, 1861-1865
> *Written by Carolyn M. Bartels*
> *Published by Two Trails Publishing*

Images of Kansas City
> *Written by William Mills*
> *Published by University of Missouri Press*

Missouri Historical Tour Guide
> *Written by D. Ray Wilson*
> *Published by Crossroads Communications*

St. Louis in the Gilded Age
> *Written by Katherine T. Corbett and Howard S. Miller*
> *Published by Missouri Historical Society Press*

The World Came to St. Louis: A Visit to the 1904 World's Fair
> *Written by Dorothy Daniels Birk*
> *Published by Chalice Press*

PHOTO ACKNOWLEDGMENTS

Grateful acknowledgment is expressed to the following for permission to reprint their photographs in "M" is for Missouri:

A — David Stradal.

B — Bob Moore.

C — Courtesy of the United States Department of the Interior; National Park Service/George Washington Carver National Monument.

D — Courtesy of the Lake of the Ozarks Convention and Visitors Bureau.

E — Courtesy of the Patee House Museum.

F — Courtesy of the Missouri Historical Society, St. Louis.

G — Courtesy of the Missouri Botanical Garden.

H — Courtesy of Mark Twain's Hannibal Convention and Visitors Bureau.

I — Monty Lyon Collection; Courtesy of the Missouri Historical Society, St. Louis.

J — Courtesy of the Missouri Historical Society, St. Louis.

K — Courtesy of the Missouri Historical Society, St. Louis.

L — Courtesy of the Missouri Historical Society, St. Louis.

M — Tim Cox.

N — Historical Collections of the Great West by Henry How; Courtesy of the Missouri Historical Society, St. Louis.

O — Courtesy of Silver Dollar City.

P — Courtesy of the Missouri Historical Society, St. Louis.

Q — Courtesy of the Jesse James Home.

R — Oscar Kuehn; Courtesy of the Missouri Historical Society, St. Louis.

S — Courtesy of the Missouri Historical Society, St. Louis.

T — Courtesy of the Harry S. Truman Library.

U — Courtesy of Silver Dollar City.

V — Courtesy of the Missouri Historical Society, St. Louis.

W — Courtesy of the Laura Ingalls Wilder Home Association/ Mansfield, Missouri.

Y — Courtesy of the Missouri Historical Society, St. Louis.

Z — David Stradal.